my MINDFUL JOURNAL

UPS!DE DOWN BOOKS

First published in Great Britain 2020 by Trigger

Trigger is a trading style of Shaw Callaghan Ltd & Shaw Callaghan 23 USA, INC.

The Foundation Centre
Navigation House, 48 Millgate, Newark
Nottinghamshire NG24 4TS UK

www.triggerpublishing.com
Copyright © 2020 Trigger Publishing
Cover art by Rebecca Prinn

British Library Cataloguing in Publication Data
A CIP catalogue record for this book is available upon request
from the British Library

ISBN: 978-1-78956-161-6

Designed by Fusion Graphic Design
Printed and bound in China
Paper from responsible sources

Illustration credits:
Terriana / iStock
Diana Vasileva / Shutterstock
@bimbimkha / Freepik

My MINDFUL JOURNAL

UPS!DE DOWN BOOKS

HOW TO USE
MY MINDFUL JOURNAL

Mindfulness means being fully present: aware of where we are and what we're doing. When we're mindful, we're less likely to get **overwhelmed**, and more likely to feel *calm* and **peaceful**.

My Mindful Journal is the perfect place to write down your thoughts, reflect on your day, plot your goals and find your calm.

To focus your mind and spark some ideas, you'll find quotes from top thinkers, philosophers and world leaders throughout the book. Mindfulness exercises, guided list-making and doodles for colouring in are sprinkled throughout like little gifts to help you grasp a moment of zen. There is plenty of space to write, so grab your favourite pen and get ready.

Now, begin your adventure toward mindfulness!

'The more you like yourself, the less you are like anyone else, which makes you unique.'

– Walt Disney, American animator and film producer

'Mindfulness isn't difficult, we just need to remember to do it.'

– Sharon Salzberg, American author

'The moment one gives close attention to anything, even a blade of grass, it becomes a mysterious, awesome, indescribably magnificent world in itself.'

– Henry Miller, American writer

'The only true wisdom is in knowing you know nothing.'

– Socrates, Greek philosopher

'It's not what happens to you, but how you react to it that matters.'

– *Epictetus, Greek philosopher*

'We humans have lost the wisdom of genuinely resting and relaxing. We worry too much. We don't allow our bodies to heal, and we don't allow our minds and hearts to heal.'

– Thích Nhất Hạnh, Vietnamese Buddhist monk and peace activist

I FEEL RELAXED WHEN I ...

1 _____

_____

2 _____

_____

3 _____

_____

4 _____

_____

5 _____

_____

'I'd rather regret the things I've done than regret the things I haven't done.'

– Lucille Ball, American actor and comedienne

'The best and safest thing is to keep a balance in your life, acknowledge the great powers around us and in us.'

– Euripides, Greek playwright

'No act of kindness, no matter how small, is ever wasted.'

– Aesop, Greek storyteller

'It doesn't matter who you are, where you come from. The ability to triumph begins with you – always.'

– Oprah Winfrey, American actor and entrepreneur

'Art is to console those who are broken by life.'

– Vincent Van Gogh, Dutch painter

'You're only given a little spark of madness.
You mustn't lose it.'

– Robin Williams, American actor and comedian

_____

_____

_____

_____

_____

_____

_____

_____

_____

_____

_____

_____

_____

_____

_____

_____

_____

_____

'Strong people don't put others down. They lift them up.'

– Michael P. Watson, British champion boxer

'I'm not perfect … But I'm enough.'

– Carl R. Rogers, American psychologist

_____

_____

_____

_____

_____

_____

_____

_____

_____

_____

_____

_____

_____

_____

_____

_____

'It's not the absence of fear. It's overcoming it. Sometimes you've got to blast through and have faith.'

– Emma Watson, British actor

'We ourselves feel that we are a drop in the ocean. But the ocean would be less because of that missing drop.'

– Mother Teresa, Catholic nun and missionary

EXERCISE: ALTERNATE NOSTRIL BREATHING

Try this breathing exercise to help you relax.

1. Sit comfortably.
2. Bring your right hand up to your nose and gently place your index and middle fingers on your forehead between your eyebrows.
3. Exhale all the way, then use your right thumb to close off your right nostril.
4. Inhale through your left nostril until you cannot take in any more breath. Then close your left nostril with your right pinky and ring fingers.
5. Remove your thumb from your right nostril and exhale all the way out.
6. Inhale through your right nostril until you cannot take in any more breath. Then close this nostril again with your thumb.
7. Release your pinky and ring fingers to open your left nostril and exhale all the way out.
8. Continue this breathing cycle for 5 minutes.

'Life is like riding a bicycle. To keep your balance, you must keep moving.'

– Albert Einstein, German physicist

'What would life be if we had no courage to attempt anything?'

– *Vincent Van Gogh*

'Only those who dare to fail greatly, can ever achieve greatly.'

– Robert F. Kennedy, American politician

'If you can't fly then run, if you can't run then walk, if you can't walk then crawl, but whatever you do you have to keep moving forward.'

– Martin Luther King Jr., American minister and civil rights activist

'I allow myself to fail. I allow myself to break. I'm not afraid of my flaws.'

– Lady Gaga, American singer and actor

MISTAKES I HAVE LEARNED FROM ...

1 _____

_____

2 _____

_____

3 _____

_____

4 _____

_____

5 _____

_____

'You may not control all the events that happen to you, but you can decide not to be reduced by them.'

– *Maya Angelou, American poet*

'At the end of the day, we can endure much more than we think we can.'

– Frida Khalo, Mexican painter

'Being deeply loved by someone gives you strength, while loving someone deeply gives you courage.'

– Lao Tzu, Chinese philosopher

'You have this one life. How do you wanna spend it? . . .
Be brave. Believe in yourself. Do what feels good. Take risks.
You have this one life. Make yourself proud.'

– Cara Delevigne, British actor and model

'Kind words can be short and easy to speak, but their echoes are truly endless.'

– Mother Teresa

_____

_____

_____

_____

_____

_____

_____

_____

_____

_____

_____

_____

_____

_____

_____

_____

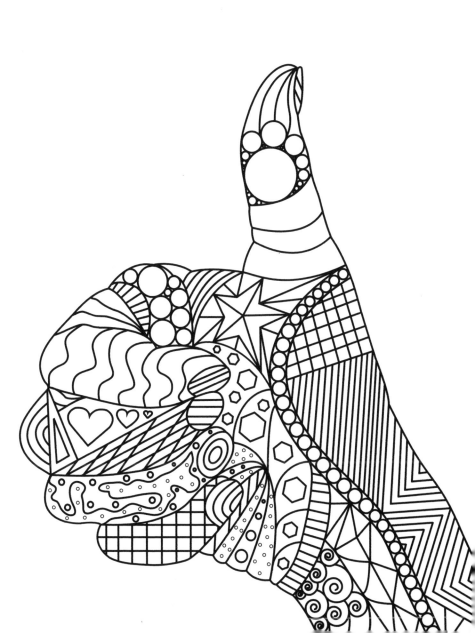

'You can't let your failures define you. You have to let your failures teach you.'

– Barack Obama,
President of the United States of America (2009 – 2017)

'Do not dwell in the past, do not dream of the future, concentrate the mind on the present moment.'

– Buddha, monk, philosopher, and founder of Buddhism

'My advice to you is not to inquire why . . .
but just enjoy your ice cream while it's on your plate.'

– Thornton Wilder, American playwright and novelist

'Be as you wish to seem.'

– Socrates

'The opportunity for [friendship] presents itself every time you meet a human being.'

– Jane Wyman, American actor

FRIENDS WHO LIFT MY SPIRITS ...

1 _____

2 _____

3 _____

4 _____

5 _____

'Swim upstream. Go the other way. Ignore the conventional wisdom.'

– Sam Walton, American businessman

'If you have the guts to keep making mistakes, your wisdom and intelligence leap forward with huge momentum.'

– Holly Near, American singer-songwriter

'Imagination is more important than knowledge.'

– Albert Einstein

'A good head and a good heart are always a formidable combination.'

– Nelson Mandela, South African revolutionary, political leader, and President of South Africa (1994 – 1999)

'There are many ways of going forward, but only one way of standing still.'

– Franklin D. Roosevelt,
President of the United States of America (1933 – 1945)

EXERCISE: BE PRESENT

Pause for a moment. Still your body and your mind. Look around you and observe.

What is in your immediate view?

What is behind you?

What is below you?

What is above you?

Use these lines to write down exactly what you see, hear, smell, and feel at this very moment.

'Friends show their love in times of trouble,
not in happiness.'

– Euripides

'Patience is the companion of wisdom.'

– Saint Augustine, Christian theologian and philosopher

'Do not go where the path may lead, go instead where there is no path and leave a trail.'

– Ralph Waldo Emerson, American author and philosopher

'Kindness is more important than wisdom, and the recognition of this is the beginning of wisdom.'

– Theodore Isaac Rubin, American psychiatrist and author

'Being entirely honest with oneself is a good exercise.'

– Sigmund Freud, Austrian neurologist and founder of psychoanalysis

'It is a common experience that a problem difficult at night is resolved in the morning after the committee of sleep has worked on it.'

– John Steinbeck, American author

'I think recharging is important, absolutely. Every now and then, you need maybe a couple of weeks to just chill out and let your emotions balance themselves out a little bit.'

– Malin Akerman, Swedish-American actor

'Doubt can motivate you, so don't be afraid of it. Confidence and doubt are at two ends of the scale, and you need both. They balance each other out.'

– *Barbra Streisand, American singer and actor*

'Do not judge me by my successes, judge me by how many times I fell down and got back up again.'

– *Nelson Mandela*

'I have just three things to teach: simplicity, patience, compassion. These three are your greatest treasures.'

– Lao Tzu

MY 'GREATEST TREASURES' ARE ...

1 _____

_____

2 _____

_____

3 _____

_____

4 _____

_____

5 _____

_____

'We are what our thoughts have made us; so, take care about what you think. Words are secondary. Thoughts live; they travel far.'

– Swami Vivekananda, Indian Hindu monk

'Be kind, for everyone you meet is fighting a hard battle.'

– Plato, Greek philosopher

'I've learned that people will forget what you said, people will forget what you did, but people will never forget how you made them feel.'

– Maya Angelou

'Peace comes from within. Do not seek it without.'

– Buddha

'Whatever the present moment contains, accept it as if you had chosen it.'

– Eckhart Tolle, German spiritual teacher and author

EXERCISE: LET IT GO

1. Either lie down or sit comfortably with your feet on the floor. Make sure you will not be interrupted during this exercise.

2. Clench your toes as much as you can and hold for 10 seconds. Then release your toes. Notice how you feel.

3. Tighten the muscles of your legs and hold for 10 seconds. Then release.

4. Continue steps 2 and 3 with each muscle group, travelling up your body: clench the muscles of your bottom, stomach, shoulders, arms, hands, and even scrunch up your face. Release each muscle group in turn, noticing exactly how you feel after you let each one go.

5. Notice which spots in your body might still feel tense, even after you release them. Repeat the exercise for these spots.

6. After you've completed the exercise, take a long moment to pause and relax. Then begin to wiggle your fingers and toes, shake your arms and legs, and stretch out your body.

7. Stand up slowly, only when you're ready.

'Give the ones you love wings to fly, roots to come back, and reasons to stay.'

– Dalai Lama, Tibetan monk and spiritual leader

'Carry out a random act of kindness, with no expectation of reward, safe in the knowledge that one day someone might do the same for you.'

– Diana, Princess of Wales

'If I cannot do great things, I can do small things in a great way.'

– Martin Luther King Jr.

'Remember that sometimes not getting what you want is a wonderful stroke of luck.'

– Dalai Lama

'The fishermen know that the sea is dangerous and the storm terrible, but they have never found these dangers sufficient reason for remaining ashore.'

— *Vincent Van Gogh*

'You'll never do a whole lot unless you're brave enough to try.'

– Dolly Parton, American singer-songwriter and actor

'Rock bottom became the solid foundation in which I rebuilt my life.'

– J.K. Rowling, British author

'Do not pray for an easy life, pray for the strength to endure a difficult one.'

– Bruce Lee, Hong Kong-American actor and martial arts expert

'However difficult life may seem, there is always something you can do and succeed at.'

– Stephen Hawking, British theoretical physicist and professor

'A hero is an ordinary individual who finds the strength to persevere and endure in spite of overwhelming obstacles.'

– Christopher Reeve, American actor (who played Superman)

MY HEROES ARE ...

1 _____

_____

2 _____

_____

3 _____

_____

4 _____

_____

5 _____

_____

'Our primary purpose is the help others. And if you can't help them, at least don't hurt them.'

– Dalai Lama

'Forgiveness liberates the soul. It removes fear. That is why it is such a powerful weapon.'

– Nelson Mandela

'We may have all come on different ships, but we're in the same boat now.'

– *Martin Luther King Jr.*

'To love is to recognize yourself in another.'

– Eckhart Tolle

'Just as treasures are uncovered from the earth, so virtue appears from good deeds, and wisdom appears from a pure and peaceful mind.'

– Buddha

WHAT BRINGS ME PEACE IS ...

1 _____

_____

2 _____

_____

3 _____

_____

4 _____

_____

5 _____

_____

'Wherever you go, there you are.'

– Jon Kabat-Zinn, American professor and founder of
Mindfulness-Based Stress Reduction method

'Be good to yourself, 'cause nobody else has the power to make you happy.'

– George Michael, British singer-songwriter

'Live the actual moment. Only this actual moment is life.'

– *Thích Nhất Hạnh*

'That's what I consider true generosity: You give your all, and yet you always feel as if it costs you nothing.'

– Simone de Beauvoir, French author and philosopher

'Do every act of your life as though it were the very last act of your life.'

— *Marcus Aurelius, Roman Emperor*

'To be a great champion you must believe you are the best. If you're not, pretend you are.'

– Muhammad Ali, American champion boxer

'Love and compassion are necessities, not luxuries. Without them, humanity cannot survive.'

– *Dalai Lama*

'Our greatest glory is not in never falling, but in rising every time we fall.'

– Confucius, Chinese philosopher and politician

'Life is a dance. Mindfulness is witnessing that dance.'

– Amit Ray, Indian author and spiritual master

'Be where you are, otherwise you will miss your life.'

– Buddha

RIGHT THIS MOMENT, I NOTICE ...

1 _____

_____

2 _____

_____

3 _____

_____

4 _____

_____

5 _____

_____

'A friend gathers all the pieces and gives them back in the right order.'

– Toni Morrison, American author and Nobel Prize winner